SCIENCE ANSWERS

Sound

FROM WHISPER TO ROCK BAND

Heinemann Library
Chicago, Illinois

Christopher Cooper

© 2004 Heinemann Library
a division of Reed Elsevier Inc.
Chicago, Illinois

Customer Service 888-454-2279

Visit our website at
www.heinemannlibrary.com

Design: Jo Hinton-Malivoire and
  Tinstar Design Ltd (www.tinstar.co.uk)
Illustrations: Jeff Edwards
Picture Research: Rosie Garai
  and Liz Eddison
Originated by Dot Gradations Ltd.
Printed in China

08 07 06 05
10 9 8 7 6 5 4 3 2

Library of Congress Cataloging-in-Publication Data|
Cooper, Christopher (Christopher Robin),
1944-
  Sound : from whisper to rock band /
Christopher Cooper.
      v. cm. -- (Science answers)
Includes bibliographical references and
index.
Contents: What is sound? -- How are
sounds made? -- How does sound travel? --
How do you change sounds? -- How do you
talk? -- How do you hear?-- How is sound
recorded?
  ISBN 1-4034-0956-0 (HC), 1-4034-3553-
7(pbk.)
 1. Sound--Juvenile literature. [1. Sound.]
I. Title. II. Series.
  QC225.5.C665 2003
  534--dc21
              2003003769

Acknowledgments
The author and publishers are grateful to the following for permission to reproduce copyright material:

p.4 Rich Meyer/Corbis; p.5 Michael Yamashita/Corbis; pp. 6, 11, 18 Photodisc; pp. 7, 13, 19, 22, 25, 27 Trevor Clifford; p.9 Steve Bronstein/Getty Images; p. 12 Steve Kaufman/Corbis; p. 14 Paul Hardy/Corbis; p. 15 Mark Thiessen/Corbis; p. 16 Barros & Barros/Getty Images; p. 17 Wilfred Krecichwost/Getty Images; p. 20 Patrick Ward/Corbis; p. 24 Joe McDonald/Corbis; p. 26 Pioneer; p. 28 Bettmann/Corbis; p. 29 Hulton Archive.

Cover photograph reproduced with permission of Photodisc.

Every effort has been made to contact copyright holders of any material reproduced in this book. Any omissions will be rectified in subsequent printings if notice is given to the publishers.

Some words are shown in bold, **like this.** You can find out what they mean by looking in the glossary

Contents

What Is Sound? 4

How Are Sounds Made? 6

How Does Sound Travel? 8

How Do You Change Sounds? 14

How Do You Talk? 20

How Do You Hear? 22

How Is Sound Recorded? 26

People Who Found the Answers 28

Amazing Facts 29

Glossary *30*

Index *32*

More Books to Read *32*

About the experiments and demonstrations

In each chapter of this book you will find a section called Science Answers. It describes an experiment or demonstration that you can try yourself. There are some simple safety rules to follow when doing an experiment:

- Ask an adult to help with any cutting using a sharp knife.
- Electrical sockets are dangerous. Never, ever try to experiment with them.
- Do not use any experimental **materials** near an electrical socket.

Materials you will use

Most of the experiments and demonstrations in this book can be done with objects you can find in your own home. A few will need items you can buy from a hardware store. You will also need paper and a pencil to record your results.

▶• What Is Sound?

Have you ever experienced complete silence? You probably have not. Even in the quietest bedroom at night, you can hear the faint **sound** of distant traffic, the rustling of trees, the wind, or the rustling of your clothes as you move.

There is always sound around you because there is always something moving nearby. And whenever anything moves, it produces sound, even if the sound is very faint. This is because sound itself is a special sort of movement—of air, water, or solid material.

Making sound

Sound is not always something that you hear coming from somewhere else. You can make sounds yourself. When you talk, you put together sounds that other people can hear and understand. **Music** consists of sounds put together in a way that is pleasant or exciting for the listener to hear. Radio and television **speakers** use electricity to create sounds.

▶•

Blocking out sounds

Your ears can detect even very quiet sounds, such as someone whispering a secret. It is hard to block sound out so that you cannot hear it at all. Even if you cover your ears, some sound travels through your body and head. It reaches the insides of your ears and can be heard—although it may be very quiet and unclear.

What is noise?

Noise can be almost any sort of sound, but the word is usually applied to unwanted or unpleasant sounds or sounds that are not speech or music that you are used to. The sounds of traffic and construction work in a city are noise. The louder they are, the worse the noise. But even your favorite music can be noise if it is distracting you while you are doing your homework. And a sound counts as noise if it is so loud that it becomes painful to hear or damages your hearing.

How Are Sounds Made?

Air is all around you. You cannot see it, but you feel it when you feel a breeze or the wind. Breezes and wind are moving air. Air is made up of huge numbers of tiny particles called **molecules.** When an object **vibrates,** or moves back and forth quickly, the air molecules around it also vibrate. Each molecule bumps into its neighbors and makes them vibrate. In this way, the vibrations spread. When air molecules in your ears start vibrating, you hear **sounds.**

All kinds of sharp movements make air molecules vibrate and create sounds. When you burst a paper bag, bang two pieces of wood together, or plunge your hand into water, the sudden, sharp movements disturb the air, making vibrations that spread outward like the ripples in the water. Molecules in solids and liquids can also vibrate, so sounds can also travel through these materials.

Can anyone hear you in space?

Sound needs something to travel through—air, water, the walls of a room. Sound travels through water even better than it travels through air. However, sound cannot travel through a vacuum. A vacuum is empty space that does not have any air molecules in it. Sound cannot reach you from the moon, sun, or any other heavenly body because the space between them and you is a vacuum.

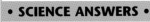

EXPERIMENT: How does a musical instrument make sound?

HYPOTHESIS
Bells, guitar strings, and drums vibrate to create sounds.

EQUIPMENT
Door-chime tubes or other type of bell, a guitar or other stringed instrument, a tambourine or small drum, rice or sugar

EXPERIMENT STEPS
1. Strike one of the tubes of the door chimes and write down how long the **note** lasts. Then gently touch it with one finger while it is still making a sound. Do you feel anything?
2. Pluck or strum the guitar string. Look at it closely. What do you see? Now touch it gently with one finger, as you did with the chime. Does the sound change? How? Why?
3. Drop grains of rice or sugar on the drum or tambourine. See how they dance about as you strike the instrument.
4. Write down what you saw.

CONCLUSION
These musical instruments vibrate when they are played. You can see and feel the vibrations, and you can hear the sound they make. The vibrations on the drum or tambourine can be strong enough to make small objects such as grains of rice or sugar move around.

How Does Sound Travel?

Vibrations in the air that you hear as **sounds** form waves. To understand what sound waves are, it is helpful to compare them with waves or ripples on the surface of water.

A ripple spreading from the middle of a pond is a **disturbance** in the water. Water does not move outward with the ripples. If you put a cork in the water, it would not be carried to the edge of the pond when the water rippled. It would instead move up and down and back and forth with the movement of the water. Each particle of water near the surface goes up and down and back and forth, in a circle. It jostles its neighbors, and these jostle their neighbors, and so the movement is passed on.

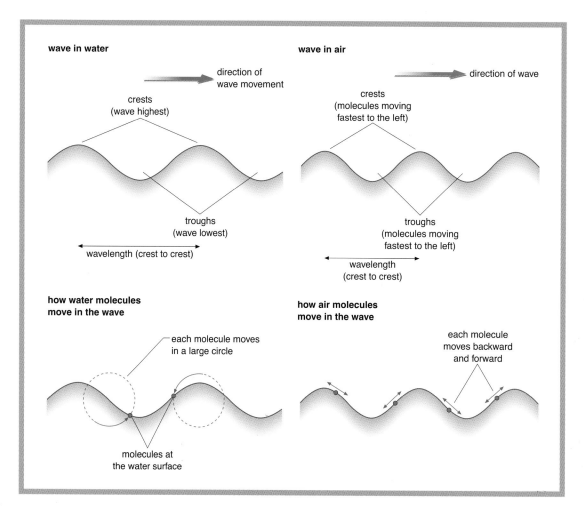

wave in water

direction of wave movement

crests (wave highest)

troughs (wave lowest)

wavelength (crest to crest)

wave in air

direction of wave

crests (molecules moving fastest to the left)

troughs (molecules moving fastest to the left)

wavelength (crest to crest)

how water molecules move in the wave

each molecule moves in a large circle

molecules at the water surface

how air molecules move in the wave

each molecule moves backward and forward

What makes a sound loud?

In a sound wave, particles of air jostle each other. The particles are **molecules,** or small groups of **atoms.** The molecules move back and forth. The distance by which a molecule moves back and forth is called the **amplitude** of its motion.

The farther the molecules move back and forth, the faster they move and the louder the sound is. This is because the molecules have a bigger effect on your ears if they move fast. But the distances the molecules move are always extremely small. You can hear sound waves in which the molecules move only a ten-millionth of an inch.

The sound of breaking glass

Sometimes sound waves can do damage, even when the sound is not very loud. Sound waves hitting a glass make it vibrate. A glass tends to vibrate at a certain number of vibrations per second. If exactly the same number of sound waves strikes the glass in each second, their effects will add together. They will make the glass vibrate so strongly that it might shatter, as this one did. For example, a singer could break a glass by singing just the right **note.**

What is wavelength?

In a wave in water, the distance from one wave crest (the highest part) to the next is called the **wavelength.** It is also the distance from one trough (deepest part) of the wave to the next. In ocean waves the wavelength can be longer than a ship. In ripples in a bath, it can be less than the tip of your finger.

In **sound** waves, the air **molecules** move only back and forth, not up and down. Strictly speaking, the sound waves do not have crests and troughs. But you can call the places where air molecules are closest together the crests of the sound waves, and the places where the molecules are farthest apart the troughs. The wavelength of a sound wave is the distance from one crest to the next, or one trough to the next. In different kinds of sound waves, wavelengths range from about 82 feet (25 meters) to less than an inch (2 1/2 centimeters).

What is frequency?

The rate at which waves pass a certain fixed point is called the **frequency** of the waves. If you watch the ocean from the end of a pier, you can count the waves that pass. Typically there might be about one every three seconds. Sound waves that humans can hear have much higher frequencies than this, ranging from about 20 waves passing per second to about 20,000. Scientists say that the frequency of sound ranges from 20 **hertz** to 20,000 hertz.

How fast can sound go?

Sound waves move at different speeds in different materials. This is because molecules can be closer together or farther apart in different substances. In solids, molecules are close together. In liquids, they are farther apart. They are farthest apart in gases. The closer together the molecules are, the easier it is for a **vibrating** molecule to disturb the molecules next to it. This makes it easier for the sound to move.

How fast do sound waves move?

Sound waves travel through air at about 1,116 feet (340 meters) per second. This is much faster than waves and ripples travel across the surface of a lake or the ocean. Light travels much faster than sound, at about 186,000 miles (300,000 kilometers) per second.

During a thunderstorm, you see the lightning before you hear the thunder. They happen at the same time, but the thunder takes longer to reach your ears.

When a ship fires a gun at sea, a double bang can often be heard. The first bang is the **sound** that has traveled through the water. The second is the sound that has traveled more slowly through the air. The speed of sound in water is about 4,900 feet (1,500 meters) per second. In air it is 1,116 feet (340 meters) per second.

How does sonar work?

Submarines and ships use **sonar** to find the positions of objects underwater.

Sonar equipment fires pulses of high-**frequency** sound waves that travel through the water. They are reflected, or bounce back, from objects such as the sea bottom or schools of fish. The sonar measures the time it takes for the reflected sound pulses to return and calculates the distance of the object.

EXPERIMENT: How does sound travel?

HYPOTHESIS
Sound consists of moving air **molecules** that push into other air molecules, moving the sound along.

EQUIPMENT
Plastic food wrap, an empty can, a little sugar, a cookie sheet, a wooden spoon

EXPERIMENT STEPS
1. Stretch the food wrap over the open end of the can and make sure it forms a tight surface like a drum.
2. Sprinkle a few grains of sugar on the plastic.
3. Hold the cookie sheet close to the can, but do not let them touch, and beat the cookie sheet very hard with the spoon. Watch the sugar grains closely. What do you see? Do you know why this happens?
4. Write down what you saw.

CONCLUSION
The sugar grains moved and bounced around. Because the only thing that happened was that a loud sound was made nearby, the sound must have caused a **disturbance** and made the grains move. The air near the sugar must have moved, and the moving air moved the sugar grains.

How Do You Change Sounds?

Sounds are not only loud or quiet; they are also high or low. The voices of children are high, and those of adults are lower. The chirp of a songbird and the jingling of sleigh bells are high; the roar of a lion and the tolling of a church bell are lower. **Pitch** is the word used to describe how low or high a sound is.

Why does the note of the siren change?

The pitch of a sound seems to change if the number of sound waves hitting your ears changes. You may have noticed this if you have heard a police car, fire engine, or ambulance driving past while sounding its **siren.** When the vehicle is coming toward you, each sound wave has a slightly shorter distance to travel to reach you than the wave before did. The time between one wave's arrival and the following wave's arrival is less than when the vehicle is not moving. The siren sounds as though it has a higher pitch.

When the vehicle is moving away from you, each wave takes longer to reach you than the one before did. The frequency seems reduced and the pitch seems lower.

What makes sounds high or low?

High-pitched sounds have high **frequencies**—many sound waves go past a fixed point each second. Low-pitched sounds have low frequencies—fewer waves go by each second. You can hear this for yourself. If you drag a stick along a railing, the separate banging sounds merge into one sound. If you drag the stick fast, you will hear a higher **note** than when you drag it slowly. The more frequently the bangs strike your ears, the higher the note you hear. In a similar way, the more often individual sound waves strike your ears, the higher the sound you hear.

Bigger means lower

These bells sound a range of notes. The biggest bells have the lowest pitch, and the smallest bells have the highest.

How do musical instruments work?

Musical instruments such as drums are designed to produce **sounds** that are loud. Instruments like violins produce long-lasting **notes**. Usually those sounds also have a definite, but easily controlled, **pitch.**

One large family of musical instruments has strings. Guitars, harps, pianos, and violins have strings or wires that **vibrate** after being plucked, struck, or stroked. While the string vibrates, it sends out sound waves. A string sounds higher if it is thinner, shorter, or more tightly stretched.

How do you get a sound by blowing?

Another large family of musical instruments is the wind instruments. They use moving air to make sound.

An instrument such as a flute or trumpet contains a column of air. Blowing into it or across the end of it causes the air inside to begin vibrating.

How do you change the pitch of a string?

A guitar has six strings of different thicknesses. They are either plucked or strummed. The guitarist gets different notes by selecting different strings and by changing the length of each string. The player does this by pressing each string down with his or her fingers at different positions along the neck of the guitar. This creates different lengths of string that the player can pluck or strum. As the length of the vibrating string is decreased, the pitch of the note climbs higher.

How do you change the pitch of the sounds that wind instruments make?

On some wind instruments, such as trumpets, there are **valves.** Pressing these valves closes off the column of air inside the instrument at various places. This makes the **vibrating** column of air longer or shorter. With other instruments, such as the flute and saxophone, the player opens and closes holes along the length of the tube. This has the same effect as making the tube longer or shorter.

EXPERIMENT: Can you make music with drinking glasses and water?

HYPOTHESIS
By striking a glass of water, you can make **music**.
The **note** made by a glass will depend on how full it is.

EQUIPMENT
A set of six or more glasses, a wooden spoon, water

EXPERIMENT STEPS
1. Pour a little water into the first glass, twice as much into the next glass, three times as much into the next, and so on until all six have water.
2. Listen to the notes that the glasses give out when you tap on them. See if you can play tunes.
3. Try tuning your glasses by comparing them with a musical instrument. Change the amount of water in each glass until the notes have the same **pitch** as the notes from the instrument.

4. Write down which glasses gave a higher **sound** and which gave a lower sound.

CONCLUSION
The more water there is in a glass, the lower the pitch of the note it gives out. More water in the glass makes the glass vibrate slower. The lower **frequency** means the pitch is lower.

How Do You Talk?

You have a combined string and wind instrument in your throat. The human voice is made when breath from the lungs passes over the **vocal cords** in the throat. The vocal cords are two small pieces of elastic tissue in the larynx, the lump at the front of the throat. Air passing over the vocal cords makes them **vibrate.** Muscles in the larynx can make them tighter to change the **pitch.** This is how you make higher and lower sounds.

Why do you need to change your speaking pitch?

The different **sounds** that make up words are mixtures of high, medium, and low sounds. You can see the importance of having all of these if you change the **tone control** on a radio or CD player. You remove the high-pitched part of the sound by turning down the **treble** control.

Why are voices so different?

This choir has singers with both low and high voices. The vocal cords of men are longer than those of women and children, and so their voices are generally deeper.

DEMONSTRATION: How speech is produced

To find out how speech is produced, follow the steps below. All you need is a magazine or a book with some text to read aloud.

DEMONSTRATION STEPS

1. Keeping your lips still and your mouth slightly open, read a few sentences from the book or magazine aloud. Which vowels and consonants sound best? Which sound worst?
2. Now press the tip of your tongue against the back of your lower front teeth to keep your tongue still while you read aloud. Press your tongue against the back of the upper front teeth and compare the result.
3. Write down what you heard.

EXPLANATION

Speech depends not only on the vocal cords but also on all the parts of the mouth working together.

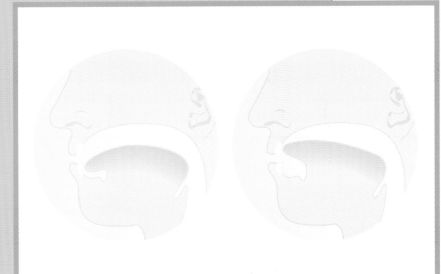

tongue against
lower teeth

tongue against
upper teeth

How Do You Hear?

You hear **sounds** through your ears. Your ears tell you not only how loud a sound is and whether it is high- or low-**pitched,** they also tell you approximately where it is coming from.

Suppose a friend standing to your left calls your name. The sound reaches your right ear less than a thousandth of a second later than it reaches the left ear. For the medium- and low-pitched parts of the sound, the brain can detect this tiny difference in arrival times and turn it into a judgment of in which direction your friend is standing.

For high-pitched sounds, the brain uses a different method. The head partly absorbs this sound, so the sound reaching the right ear is less loud. The brain uses the difference in loudness to help figure out from where the sound is coming.

What happens inside the ear?

A complicated pathway leads from the outer ear to the brain. Sounds enter the ear canal and strike a piece of thin tissue called the eardrum, making it **vibrate.** These vibrations pass along a chain of three small bones—the hammer, anvil, and stirrup. Next they enter a complicated fluid-filled spiral structure, the cochlea. Here, tiny hairlike cells begin to vibrate. Finally, nerve signals travel from the cells to the brain along the auditory nerve. The brain interprets these as sounds.

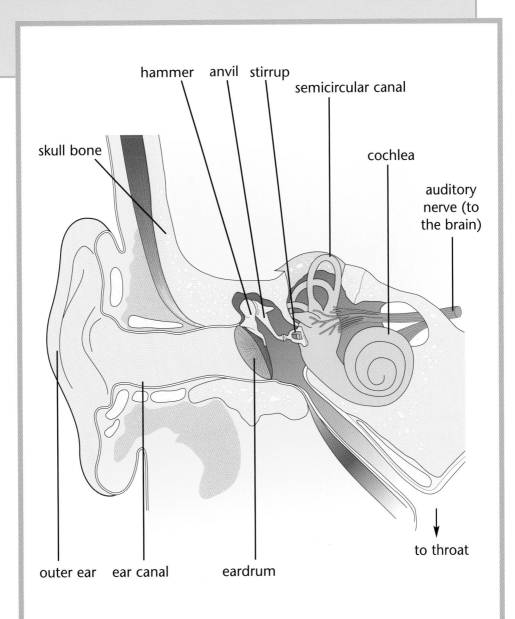

hammer anvil stirrup

semicircular canal

skull bone

cochlea

auditory nerve (to the brain)

to throat

outer ear   ear canal   eardrum

Do animals hear things differently?

Many animals have better **hearing** than humans do. Dogs have very sensitive hearing. They often get excited by hearing someone approaching the family house well before their owner can hear anything.

Dogs can hear higher-**pitched sounds** than humans can. Some dog owners use **ultrasonic** whistles. These are so high-pitched that humans cannot hear them.

Elephants can hear low-**frequency** sounds, down to about five **hertz.** Compare this to twenty hertz, which is the lowest that most humans can hear.

Why do bats have such big ears?

Bats use sound as a kind of radar. A bat sends out high-pitched squeaks at frequencies as high as 200,000 hertz. These sounds bounce off objects and are picked up by the bat's big, sensitive ears. Bats can avoid obstacles and catch flying insects in the dark thanks to these **echoes.**

INVESTIGATION: Why do you hear sounds differently?

The sounds you hear are affected when they pass through matter. You can test this for yourself by following the steps below. You will need a cassette recorder and tape. Pay careful attention to how your voice sounds in the three different situations.

INVESTIGATION STEPS
1. Speak a few words aloud in the ordinary way.
2. Repeat the words with your hands pressed firmly over both ears. Do you sound the same or different?
3. **Record** yourself saying the same words and play back the tape. Does your recorded voice sound the same or different from either of the first two tests?
4. Write down how your voice sounded in each test.

EXPLANATION
Your voice should have sounded different in each test. In the first test, what you heard consisted partly of sound that had traveled through the air to reach your ears and partly of sound that had traveled through your head. In the second test, you heard sound that traveled only through your head. In the third test, you heard sound as it reached the **microphone** after traveling only through the air. This is what other people hear when you speak.

How Is Sound Recorded?

CDs and cassette tapes store **sounds** in the form of a "picture" of the sound wave. A CD or tape player translates this "picture" back into a sound that is a copy of the original.

A CD is a metal disk coated in transparent protective plastic. On one side of the metal there is a spiral track, which is a series of tiny pits separated by gaps called flats. The pits and flats are of variable sizes. The pattern of pits and flats is a code that represents the loudness and **pitch** of the sound at each moment. The CD player reads the pattern of pits and flats and turns them into alterations in the strength of an electric current. The current goes from the CD player to **speakers.**

An audiocassette tape consists of a metal-coated plastic tape. The metal is magnetized. The strength of the magnetization varies along the tape, according to the loudness of the sound at the corresponding moment.

INVESTIGATION: How can a sound be sent over a distance?

To show how you can send speech over a distance, follow the steps below. You will need two empty plastic yogurt containers and six to nine feet (two to three meters) of string.

INVESTIGATION STEPS

1. Carefully pierce a hole in the bottom of each yogurt container and thread one end of the string through. Tie a knot to keep the string from sliding out.
2. While a friend holds one container, take the other and stretch the string tightly between you.
3. Talk softly into your container while your friend holds the other container to his or her ear. Taking turns, see if you can hear each other and carry on a conversation.
4. Write down what happened.

EXPLANATION

A tightly stretched string can carry a human voice. In your string phone, the **vibrations** in the air caused by your voice make the yogurt container vibrate. This in turn makes the string vibrate. The vibrations of the string make the other yogurt container vibrate. This causes the air to vibrate as sounds that your friend can hear.

People Who Found the Answers

Marin Mersenne (1588-1648)

The **pitch** of a string is lower for strings that are longer, heavier, or stretched less tightly. French scientist and monk Marin Mersenne summed this up in three laws named after him. He counted the **vibrations** of very long, very slowly vibrating strings and used the laws to calculate how fast the strings of musical instruments vibrate.

Mersenne also made a fairly accurate measurement of the speed of **sound** by measuring the time required for an **echo** to return when sound was reflected from an obstacle at a known distance.

Thomas Alva Edison (1847-1931)

The modern world is dominated by moving pictures, **recorded** sound, telephones, and electric power. All of these things were either invented or improved by Thomas Edison.

Edison was a telegraph operator. He invented several improvements, including a printing telegraph, which made a printed record of each message.

Edison became a full-time inventor and set up his own laboratory. He invented the sort of telephone **microphone** that is still used today. It improved the sound of Alexander Graham Bell's telephone invention.

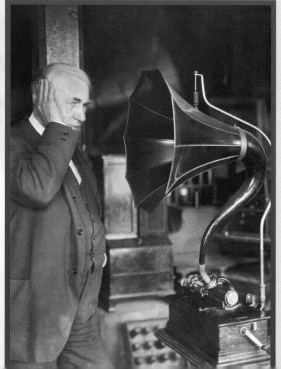

In 1877, Edison invented the first phonograph for recording and replaying sound. Later, he made the first talking pictures by linking a phonograph with a film projector.

Amazing Facts

- During World War II, enemy aircraft were detected at a distance by giant mechanical "ears." They consisted of large dishes that collected the faint sounds of enemy aircraft and focused them onto microphones.

- The loudest sound ever heard was the explosion of the volcano of Krakatoa in 1883. This uninhabited island in the Pacific blew up, raising a wave that drowned 36,000 people on other islands. The sound was so loud it could be heard in Australia, 1,864 miles (3,000 kilometers) away.

- **Ultrasound** is beamed into trees to discover disease deep within the trunk. The sound waves are affected differently by empty spaces in the wood, by unhealthy parts, and by parts that have rotted away.

- Hundreds of species of fish make sounds. Some make sounds using their swim-bladder, a gas-filled bag in the fish's body that controls how buoyant the fish is. For example, cusk eels drum on the swim-bladder with a special bone. Dolphins and whales locate prey and each other by sending out clicks from the front of their heads.

 # Glossary

amplitude measure of how fast the molecules of air vibrate back and forth when they are disturbed. The bigger the amplitude, the louder the sound.

atom tiny particle of matter too small to be seen without a powerful microscope

disturbance movement or other change of something that was at rest

echo sound that bounces off something before reaching a listener

frequency how often something happens in one second

hearing ability of animals and human beings to detect sound

hertz basic unit of frequency, symbol Hz. If 200 sound waves pass a particular point every second, the sound has a frequency of 200 Hz.

microphone device that detects sounds and can be used for recording, amplifying, or broadcasting

molecule two or more atoms linked together

music sounds made by human beings and arranged to be pleasing or exciting

noise any sound, but especially one that is not wanted because it is loud, unpleasant, or out of place

note single musical sound with a definite pitch

pitch how high or low a sound is

recording pattern of magnetism on a magnetic tape or of pits in a plastic disk (CD), which is a "picture" of a particular sound. The recording can be used to produce sound that is a copy of the original.

siren device that makes a very loud warning sound

sonar method of using sound to find objects underwater. A sonar device on a ship or submarine sends out sound waves that are reflected by objects such as the seafloor, schools of fish, or other submarines. A computer in the sonar device turns the echoes into a picture of the surroundings.

sound vibrations of molecules that travel through air, water, or solid materials

speaker device that produces sound using the electric current from a radio, CD player, TV set, or other such device

tone control control on a radio, tape player, CD player, or other sound system that alters the amount of high- or low-frequency sound

treble high-pitched part of a sound, especially music or the sound from a radio or CD player

ultrasound sound of a very high frequency of 20,000 hertz and above

valve on a musical wind instrument, a device that when pressed changes the length of the tubing through which air is blown. This allows the player to produce a different range of notes.

vibrate move rapidly in a back-and-forth motion

vocal cords two pieces of elastic tissue in the larynx, which is the lump at the front of the throat. The vocal cords vibrate when air from the lungs passes over them, producing many of the sounds of speech.

wavelength distance from one crest of a wave to the next. In the case of a sound wave, a crest is a place where the vibrating molecules are moving fastest, either forward or backward.

 # Index

air disturbances 6, 8, 13
amplitude 9
animals 24, 29
audiocassette tapes 26

bats 24
bells 15

ears 22–23, 24
echoes 24, 28
Edison, Thomas Alva 28

fish 29
frequencies 10, 14, 15, 19, 24

glasses 9, 19
guitars 7, 16, 17

hearing 22–25
hertz 10, 24
human voice 20–21, 25, 27

Mersenne, Marin 28
microphones 25, 28
molecules 6, 9, 10, 13
musical instruments 7, 16–18, 28

notes, musical 15, 16, 19

pitch 14, 15, 16, 17, 19, 20, 22, 28

recording sounds 26

sirens 14
sonar 12
sound waves 8–11, 12, 15, 16, 29
space 6
speech 20–21, 25, 27
speed of sound 11, 12, 28

ultrasound 24, 29

valves 18
vibrations 6, 7, 8, 9, 16, 17, 18, 19, 20, 23, 27, 28
vocal cords 20

wavelength 10
wind instruments 18

More Books to Read

Nankivell-Aston, Sally and Dorothy Jackson. *Science Experiments with Sound.* Danbury, Conn.: Scholastic Library Publishing, 2000.

Parker, Steve. *Science Fact Files: Light and Sound.* Austin, Tex.: Raintree, 2000.

Searle, Bobbi *Fascinating Science Projects: Sound.* Brookfield, Conn.: Millbrook Press, Inc., 2002.